DREAM TO WIN OLYMPIC GOLD

Rebecca Adlington

Roy Apps

Illustrated by Chris King

EDGE FRANKLIN WATTS

LONDON·SYDNEY

Chapter One:

Double Silver!

The 14-year-old girl stood on the side of the Olympic-sized swimming pool in Paris. She looked around her. All the other girls were older and bigger than her. She wasn't too worried though.

She was used to being the youngest. She had two older sisters, both of whom were good swimmers. Ever since she had started swimming at the age of six, she had been trying to catch them up.

But this was the final of the 2003 European Youth Olympics 800 metres freestyle.

5

As the swimmers dived in, the arena echoed noisily with shouts and cheers from the spectators.

"Come on, Becks!" shouted the girl's family from their seats in the crowd. "You can do it!"

As the swimmers reached the end of the race, the cheering and shouting got louder. The 14-year-old girl touched the finishing wall in second place. She had swum the race of her life.

Afterwards, as all her family and friends crowded round to congratulate her for winning the silver medal, she felt a bit shell-shocked. She looked up and saw a man she did not recognise approaching them. Her mum turned towards him.

"That was a brilliant race your daughter swam," he said. "I think she's got the potential to go to the very top. My name's Bill Furniss, by the way. I'm a professional swimming coach and I'd like to offer to coach your daughter."

The young swimmer and her mum had no trouble accepting Bill Furniss's offer. His club was in Nottingham, only about half an hour's drive from their home in Mansfield.

It would have been nice to have gone out that evening to celebrate, but there was another final to prepare for: the 400 metres freestyle.

The young British swimmer won a silver medal in that race, too. The crowd cheered as she stood on the podium and once again the race organiser declared:

"Silver medal, Rebecca Adlington, Great Britain!"

Chapter Two:

Tough Training

Becky woke up to the sound of her mum's voice: "Come on, Becks love, get up! We'll be late!"

Becky groaned, turned over and pulled the bed covers over her head. She half-opened one eye and peered at her bedside clock. It was just gone 5am.

She groaned again, staggered out of bed and stumbled out of her bedroom into the bathroom.

Twenty minutes later she was sitting in her mum's car on the way to the pool. Outside it was dark and frosty. There were few other cars on the road. No wonder – there weren't many people up at that time of the morning.

Becky fiddled with the car radio, switching it from station to station.

"Can't you leave it on one channel?" sighed Becky's mum.

"I've got to find a song I like," said Becky. "I need a happy song in my head when I swim."

Becky knew that if she was going to achieve her dream of becoming a world-class swimmer, early morning swims every day before school were a necessary part of her training. She swam for two hours before school and had her breakfast out of a lunch box in the car going from the pool to school.

Then she trained again after school, doing her homework in the car on the way home, before finally crashing into bed after her dinner. Going to bed early was a part of her training.

Becky looked out of the car window. They were nearly at the pool.

Her friends thought she was crazy.

"I don't know how you do it, Becky," one of them had told her the other day.

"I just love swimming," Becky answered.

"So, you won't be coming to Rachel's party tonight?"

Becky shook her head. "I'd love to, but it's Saturday tomorrow, and I've still got to be up early for training."

Becky's mum drove into the swimming pool car park. Becky thought back to the first time they had been here to Nova Centurion – Bill Furniss's club. Becky and Bill had sat down for a chat in the café at the pool. The TV had been on in the corner, showing a football match.

"There's your first lesson," Bill had told her, nodding in the direction of the TV. "Swimming isn't like football. Footballers train a few times a week. Look at them on the pitch, they stop and start; have a bit of a rest…"

Becky looked at the screen and saw what Bill meant.

"Swimming is an endurance sport," he went on, "it's about how fast you can swim, to the hundredth of a second. You're full speed for the whole of the race, and the only way to train is to practise racing again and again, as fast as you can."

Becky soon found out endurance training
was hard work – and it hurt. It meant
pushing her heart rate close to the maximum
until her muscles screamed in agony.

A year after she started being coached by
Bill Furniss, Becky won the 800 metres
freestyle gold medal at the European Junior
Championships in Portugal, beating her
own personal best time.

Bill Furniss was thrilled. "There's no reason why you shouldn't get gold at the senior European Championships next year," he told Becky. "You've got the talent and the determination to make 2005 your best year ever."

But that was where he was wrong.

Chapter Three:

Shattered Dream

As usual, Becky woke up to the sound of her mum's voice: "Come on, Becks love! Time to get up!"

As usual, Becky groaned, turned over and pulled the bed covers over her head.

As usual, she half-opened one eye and peered at her bedside clock. It was just gone 5am. She sat up and got out of bed. Suddenly, she realised, something was wrong. Her legs didn't feel right. They seemed heavy and very, very tired.

Somehow she managed to dress and get downstairs and into the car.

Swimming that morning was awful. Becky could hardly manage one length.

"I just feel so tired," she told Bill Furniss.

"You've not got the flu, have you?" he asked.

"Probably," Becky replied. "I have got a bit of a sore throat."

Over the next few weeks, Becky's sore throat got better, but the tiredness got worse.

Becky's mum took her to see the doctor.

"I think you've got glandular fever," the doctor said. "It's a viral infection that causes extreme tiredness."

Becky's mum nodded. "Yes, I know what glandular fever's like," she said. "Becky's older sister Chloe had it. She had to give up her swimming for months."

"But Mum, I've got the European Championships to train for!" Becky was close to tears.

"I'm sorry," the doctor said. "If you exercise heavily while you've got glandular fever you could damage your spleen, and that would be very serious."

"How long will it be until I get better?" asked Becky in a quiet voice.

The doctor shrugged. "Most patients start to feel better in a few weeks," he replied.

"Others need two or three months, sometimes even longer."

Becky sat in stunned silence. Weeks – let alone months – of not being able to train meant that her dream of competing in the 2005 European Championships was over. And if she wasn't training, she wouldn't need a coach.

It felt like the end of the world.

Chapter Four:

Keeping the Feel of the Water Going

They drove to the pool so that Becky could tell Bill Furniss the bad news. As she walked up the steps to the office, she watched sadly as the swimmers below her powered their way through the water.

Bill Furniss listened calmly as Becky spoke. "So you see, I won't be doing any competitive swimming for a while," she explained. She got up to leave. "But thanks for all that you've done for me, Bill. You've been a fantastic coach."

"Whoa!" said Bill. "Not so fast. Where are you going?"

"Home," said Becky. "Mum's waiting for me downstairs."

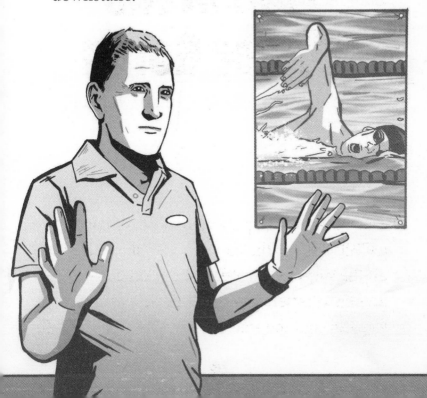

"Listen," said Bill. "Even if you've got glandular fever, you have to keep swimming. That way you keep the feel of the water going. If you don't, you'll lose your technique. I'll meet your doctor to see what we can sort out."

"You mean you'll still go on doing my coaching?" asked Becky, sounding surprised.

"Of course," said Bill. "It's disappointing about the European Championships. But there's always next year."

Bill Furniss sat down with Becky's doctor and together they worked out a gentle swimming programme for her.

It wasn't easy. The glandular fever made Becky feel heavy, like she was carrying weights around. And although she was sleeping 12 hours a night, she always felt very, very tired. But Bill Furniss made sure she didn't overdo it, and as for Becky, she was just pleased that she'd not had to give up swimming.

Gradually, Becky began to feel stronger and was able to swim just a little more each time. Perhaps, thought Becky, I'll soon be able to focus on my dream of becoming a world-class swimmer, once again.

But the Adlington household still wasn't the cheeriest place.

Becky's sister Laura had caught glandular fever, too.

"Ah well," joked Mrs Adlington. "They say it runs in families, and as Chloe and Becky have both had it, I guess it's Laura's turn."

One morning before school, Becky popped her head into Laura's bedroom. Laura lay still in her bed, her eyes half-closed. "Don't worry, you'll start to feel better in a week or two. I did," Becky said. Laura didn't reply.

At school, Becky tried to concentrate on lessons, but she couldn't help thinking about Laura. She was sure her sister had looked a lot worse than she had when she first had the illness.

After school, Becky stood in the reception area, waiting for her mum to pick her up for her training session. She looked at her watch and frowned. Her mum was late – and that was odd. She checked her mobile. There were no messages.

Suddenly, she saw a van racing up the school drive; bouncing over the speed humps. It was her dad's van. Why wasn't he at work?

As he pulled up in front of the school, she dashed out to meet him.

"Dad? What's happened?" she asked him, already sensing something was seriously wrong.

"They've taken Laura to the hospital," Becky's dad explained. "Her glandular fever's taken a turn for the worse. It's caused her brain to start to swell. She's in intensive care."

Chapter Five:

Family Comes First

Becky looked down at Laura lying still and silent in her hospital bed. She didn't seem to be a person at all, but part of all the machinery surrounding her.

At that moment, nothing else in Becky's world; friends, school – not even swimming – mattered. All that Becky wanted was for her sister to get better.

Becky's mum and dad were at the hospital most of the time Laura was there, so Becky's eldest sister Chloe took over running the house and taking Becky to training.

Gradually, Laura began to get better. By the time the trials for the 2006 Commonwealth Games in Australia came round, Laura was out of danger and Becky was almost fully fit.

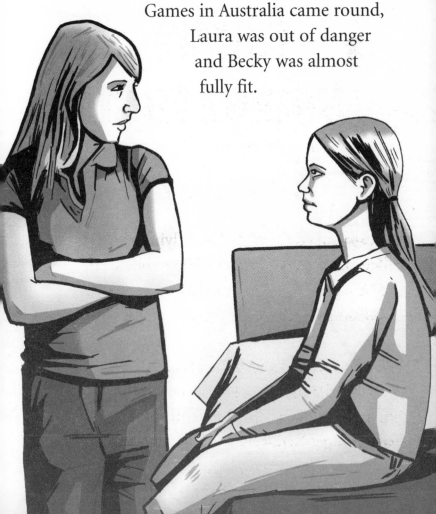

Becky swam a good race, feeling better than she had for months and powering her way to a strong finish. But it wasn't quite good or strong enough. She missed selection for the Commonwealth Games by 0.02 seconds.

Becky was heart-broken. Would she ever be a top swimmer? Or would it be better to give up now?

Bill Furniss took her to one side and said: "Don't look so down. You've got just over two years to prepare and train for the big one."

Becky stared at him. "You mean the Olympic Games?"

Bill Furniss nodded. "You've got the talent and the determination to become an Olympic Champion. I've always believed that and I know, deep down, you have, too. You can't give up the dream now."

Gradually, things returned to normal in the Adlington household. Laura came home from hospital and Becky's training programme returned to its usual routine. But when it came to actual races, Becky had her ups and downs. She won silver at the 2006 European Championships in her favourite race; the 800 metres freestyle. But she came a miserable tenth in the same race in the 2007 World Championships.

In order to go to the 2008 Olympic Games, Becky had to get a good time at the British Olympic trials. Becky's mum had never seen her daughter looking so nervous.

"Don't worry. You'll get through," her mum said. "And when you're in Beijing, all the family will be there to cheer you on! Your dad and I bought tickets for the 800 metre finals six months ago."

Becky was speechless. If her family believed in her that much, then she just had to get through.

And she did. She won the 200 metres, 400 metres and 800 metres freestyle trials. She was on her way to Beijing, China to swim in not just the 800 metres, but the 400 metres, too.

Chapter Six:

Double Gold!

The Olympic 400 metres freestyle was the first race Becky had swum where her mum had not been watching.

Her family had bought tickets just for the 800 metres; they had no reason to think that Becky would be swimming the 400 metres as well. It wasn't a distance she had swum at international level before.

The Adlington house was packed with friends and relatives, all crowding round the TV. Becky wasn't expected to win a medal; after all, this wasn't her specialist distance, but it would be good practice for the 800 metres, they thought.

As the swimmers touched the side for the final lap, everybody watching realised that Becky might win a medal. Shouts, screams and cheers filled the room. As the race ended, it was difficult to tell whose hand had touched the wall first.

There was a moment's silence as the camera moved up to the scoreboard. Then the result flashed up: Gold: Rebecca Adlington by 0.07 seconds! The Adlington house erupted.

Once Becky was out of the pool, the first person she saw was Bill Furniss. She was still breathless and lost for words. Bill Furniss wasn't: "Congratulations," he said. "Rebecca Adlington: Olympic Champion."

A few days later, Becky's family arrived to see her in the 800 metres. For Becky, the 800 metres was the big race, the one she really cared about. But would she be able to manage it?

On the day of the race, she was tired. Winning the 400 metres had taken a lot out of her. She felt tearful, faint and sick.

When it was time to go to the pool, she had to lie down on the floor just to try and relax. Eventually, she managed to get up and make her way to the swimming pool.

Once Becky dived into the water though, all the worry, tiredness and panic disappeared. Every minute – every second – of the race, she pushed herself harder than she had ever pushed herself before, until pain seared through every muscle in her body. She just had to get gold!

She swam the last lap and her hand touched the wall. Had she done it?

As she climbed out of the water, her body ached so much that she couldn't stand. She collapsed at the side of the pool. Gradually, her head cleared and she heard shouts and cheers echoing around the arena.

She had won gold! Not only that, she had beaten the 19-year-old world record for the women's 800 metres freestyle. Rebecca Adlington, double gold medalist, had finally achieved her dream.

 Full name: Rebecca Adlington

 Born: Mansfield, Notts, 17 February 1989

1994	Begins swimming aged 5
1999	Starts swimming competitively at Sherwood Colliery Swimming Club in Mansfield, Nottinghamshire
2001	National Age Group Championships 800m Freestyle Gold medal
2003	European Youth Olympic Festival, Paris: Silver medalist 400m and 800m Freestyle. Teams up with coach Bill Furniss at the Nova Centurion Club
2004	European Junior Championships: 800m Freestyle Gold medal
2006	British Championships: 800m Freestyle Gold medal
2008	British Championships: 200m Freestyle: Gold medal, 400m Freestyle: Gold medal, 800m Freestyle: Gold medal
2008	Olympic Games, Beijing: 400m Freestyle: Gold medal, 800m Freestyle: Gold medal (World Record). First British Olympic swimming champion since 1988; first British swimmer to win two Olympic Gold medals since 1908; most successful British Olympic swimmer for 100 years
2008	Sports Journalists' Association Sportswoman of the Year. Receives her trophy at a ceremony in the City of London from HRH the Princess Royal
2009	Receives the OBE from the Queen at Buckingham Palace

"Big Ears! Big Ears!"

The boy they called Big Ears squirmed in his seat, desperately trying to turn away from the taunting.

Then he looked up and caught the glint of evil triumph in the face of the pink, freckly boy, who was behind him.

Suddenly, something inside him snapped. He turned around and thumped the freckly boy. Then he thumped him again and again, his anger and hurt feeding every punch.

Around him the chants of "Big Ears!" quickly turned to cries of: "Fight! Fight!"

**Continue reading this story in
DREAM TO WIN: Michael Phelps**

DREAM
TO WIN
OLYMPIC GOLD

Michael
Phelps

Roy Apps

Also by Roy Apps,
published by Franklin Watts:

978 0 7496 7057 3

978 0 7496 7056 6

978 0 7496 7054 2

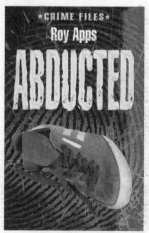

978 0 7496 7053 5